From Egg to Adult
The Life Cycle of Fish

Heinemann
LIBRARY

Richard and Louise Spilsbury

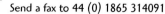

www.heinemann.co.uk/library

Visit our website to find out more information about **Heinemann Library** books.

To order:
☎ Phone 44 (0) 1865 888066
▤ Send a fax to 44 (0) 1865 314091
💻 Visit the Heinemann Bookshop at www.heinemann.co.uk/library to browse our catalogue and order online.

First published in Great Britain by Heinemann Library, Halley Court, Jordan Hill, Oxford OX2 8EJ, part of Harcourt Education Ltd. Heinemann is a registered trademark of Harcourt Education Ltd.

Editorial: Nicole Irving and Georga Godwin
Design: Jo Hinton-Malivoire and AMR
Illustrations: David Woodroffe
Picture Research: Maria Joannou and Liz Eddison
Production: Séverine Ribierre

Originated by Dot Gradations Ltd
Printed in China by Wing King Tong

ISBN 0 431 16862 8
07 06 05 04 03
10 9 8 7 6 5 4 3 2 1

British Library Cataloguing in Publication Data
Spilsbury, Richard and Spilsbury, Louise
From egg to adult: The life cycle of fish
571.8'117
A full catalogue record for this book is available from the British Library.

Acknowledgements
The publishers would like to thank the following for permission to reproduce photographs: Bruce Coleman p. **17**; Bruce Coleman Collection/Jeff Foott p. **25**; Bruce Coleman Collection/Kim Taylor p. **5**; Corbis/Natalie Fobes pp. **9**, **26a**; Corbis pp. **19**, **28**; FLPA/C. J. Swale p. **20**; FLPA/D. P. Wilson p. **24**; Heather Angel p. **8**; NHPA p. **7**; NHPA/Ant Photo Library pp. **12**, **15**; NHPA/Kevin Schafer p. **22**; NHPA/Lutra p. **4**; NHPA/Trevor Mcdonald p. **26b**; Oxford Scientific Films p. **27**; Oxford Scientific Films/Breck P. Kent p. **10**; Oxford Scientific Films/Clive Bromhall p. **21**; Oxford Scientific Films/Colin Milkins p. **13**; Oxford Scientific Films/David Fleetham p. **14**; Oxford Scientific Films/Howard Hall p. **23**; Oxford Scientific Films/Ian Root p. **18**; Oxford Scientific Films/Karen Gowlett-Holmes p. **16**; Oxford Scientific Films/Rodger Jackman p. **6**; SPL p. **11**.

Cover photograph of the golden Mozambique mouth brooder, reproduced with permission of Oxford Scientific Films.

The authors would like to thank their teachers for all their help and support.

The fish at the top of each page is a blue French angelfish.

The Publishers would like to thank Colin Fountain for his assistance in the preparation of this book.

Every effort has been made to contact copyright holders of any material reproduced in this book. Any omissions will be rectified in subsequent printings if notice is given to the Publishers.

Contents

Look but don't touch: many fish are delicate and some are dangerous. If you see one in the wild, do not approach too close. Look at it but do not try to touch it!

Any words appearing in bold, **like this**, are explained in the Glossary.

What is a fish?

There are around 23,000 different **species** (kinds) of fish in the world. Although they may look very different, they share certain features that make them all fish. All fish are vertebrates (animals with backbones). They live in water and breathe through special body parts called **gills**. Fish are cold-blooded. That means they cannot control their body temperature – it changes as the temperature of the water around them changes.

*This is a perch, one of the most common kinds of fish. Like most fish, it is covered with **scales** that **protect** its body.*

Where do fish live?

All fish live in water. Water is harder to move through than air, so fish are shaped to help them swim. Most are streamlined – they have smooth body shapes that can move through water quickly. They swim by moving their bodies from side to side. Their **fins** are used for braking and keep them upright and steady.

How are fish born?

The majority of baby fish **hatch** from eggs laid by their mother. A **female** fish produces hundreds of eggs at a time, but the number depends on her fitness and the **species** she belongs to. Sticklebacks usually lay around 200 eggs, but turbots may lay 9 million eggs.

This picture of a fish egg has been magnified (made bigger) so you can see the embryo inside.

What's in a fish egg?

The baby fish growing inside an egg is called an **embryo**. Fish eggs, like those of other animals, contain a bag of food called the **yolk**. The embryo uses this food to give it **energy** to grow bigger and stronger. Fish eggs do not have a shell like bird or reptile eggs. Most fish eggs have a thin coating, which provides little **protection** for the growing embryo.

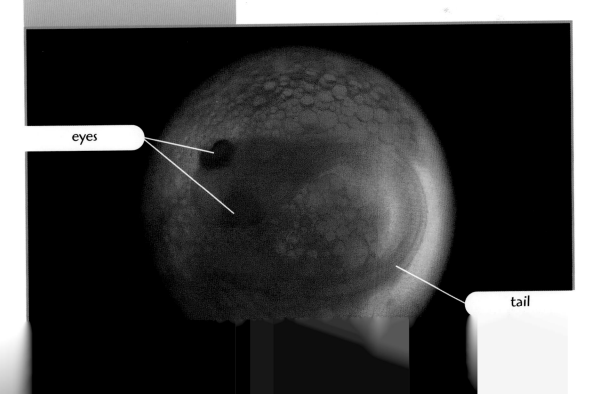

eyes

tail

Where are fish born?

Almost all fish eggs hatch in water. Some float one by one at the water surface and are spread by the tides. Others are sticky and sink to the water bottom where they stick to plants and rocks. Some fish lay their eggs in big clumps or in sticky strings.

Pacific herrings lay their sticky eggs in shallow water in spring. These eggs are stuck to seaweed.

Odd ones out

Some fish, such as guppies, do not lay eggs. They give birth to young fish, not eggs. The embryos develop and the eggs hatch inside the female's body. Because there is not much room inside a fish's body, these fish have only a few young at a time.

How long does hatching take?

Embryos of different fishes take different lengths of time to develop before they are ready to hatch. Most fish eggs hatch after about two months, but some tropical fish eggs hatch after only a day or two. Shark eggs can take up to five months. The speed can depend on water temperature – if the same kinds of eggs are laid in warmer water, they hatch more quickly than those in colder water.

How do fish hatch out?

When the embryo inside an egg is fully developed, it wriggles and squirms until it breaks open its egg's coating. A newly hatched fish is often called a **fry**. Fry of many types of fish often hatch around the same time because their eggs were laid at the same time.

Brown trout fry, like this one, are ready to hatch two to four months after their eggs are laid.

7

Who looks after baby fish?

Most fish never see their parents. After laying their eggs the parents swim away and have nothing more to do with them. The **fry** that **hatch** out have to look after themselves. Newly hatched fish are usually very small. Adult plaice are about 50 cm long, but their fry only measure 6.5 mm. They are not very strong, and the **muscles** and **fins** that will help them swim are not fully grown yet.

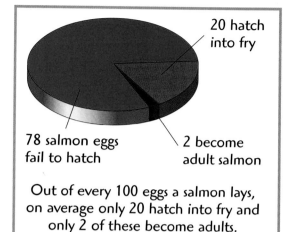

20 hatch into fry

78 salmon eggs fail to hatch

2 become adult salmon

Out of every 100 eggs a salmon lays, on average only 20 hatch into fry and only 2 of these become adults.

*Most fry, like this one, do not survive for many days after hatching because of **predators**.*

Count down!

There is an important reason why fish lay so many eggs. The fry that hatch out are often very small and predators feed on them in large numbers. By laying lots of eggs, at least a few fry should survive to grow into adults.

Life alone is risky

Life is dangerous for young fish. Because they cannot swim well they may be washed into colder waters or away from food. This also makes them easy to catch and many different predators, including insects, fish, birds and frogs, try to eat them. Many kinds of fish fry swim to hiding places to avoid being spotted.

Model parents

Some fish do look after their fry. After she lays her eggs, the female tilapia takes them into her mouth. The eggs hatch and the fry stay safely inside until they are big enough to look after themselves. The males of a few **species**, such as some sticklebacks, guard their fry for a short time after they have hatched.

Coho salmon hatch at night. This gives them the chance to swim to the shelter of shady pools and banks before daylight. Here they can feed hidden from predators.

How do baby fish grow bigger?

Young fish need to eat food to get the **energy** their bodies need to grow bigger. When most fish first **hatch** out, they look quite different to the adult. Many have unformed **fins** and they still have a **yolk** sac attached to their stomach. They use food from this sac until it has all gone. By this time they are able to find food for themselves.

The fins on this newly hatched trout have not formed properly yet and it has a yolk sac on its stomach. The yolk lasts until the fins are fully-grown. This takes about three to four months.

Name-calling

People give fish particular names for the different stages of growth. When salmon hatch out they are called alevins. At four to six weeks old, they start to eat insect **larvae**, and become **fry**. Two years later they develop stripes and are called parrs. After another two years they lose the stripes and become silver smolts. As adults, they are reddish-brown with red and black spots.

First foods

Young fish usually eat small bits of food that float in the water. This food may be tiny plants and insect eggs or larvae (newly hatched insects). As they get bigger, fish need to eat larger amounts of food. Young anglerfish live at the surface of the sea at first, eating **plankton**. When they become adults they move to the deep sea, to eat other fish and squid.

Some fish eat plankton all their lives, from egg to adult – they just eat a lot more of it as they grow. Plankton eaters include two of the biggest fish of all – the basking shark and the whale shark. These huge fish swim along with their mouths open catching tonnes of plankton.

Many baby fish that live in the sea eat tiny floating animals, like these, called copepods. There are several different types of copepod, but most are less than one millimetre long.

The whale shark is a massive plankton eater with a bathtub-sized mouth. As it swims, hundreds of litres of water containing floating plankton go into its mouth and pass over its **gills**. Rows of bristles called gill rakers trap the plankton that is swallowed.

On the menu

Some of the fish that live in rivers and streams eat plants that grow on the banks and river bottoms. Others eat the small animals that feed on those plants, such as snail and worms, or insects and other fish. Out in the deep oceans and seas there are no plants to eat, so most fish are **carnivores**. Some feed on plankton, others eat shrimps, crabs and **shellfish** or other fish.

Hunters

Most fish that are carnivores hunt for their **prey**. Tuna and barracuda swim very fast into large **shoals** of fish to capture a meal. Swordfish spear and slash their prey with a snout that is so long and pointed it looks like a sword. Electric eels stun their prey with electric shocks. Pike hide amongst weeds and charge out to catch prey with their sharp teeth.

Pike eat almost anything they can catch – fish, frogs, birds and sometimes even young otters.

Unusual food

Some fish are **scavengers**. They do not catch their own meals, but eat dead animals that sink down to the seabed. Hagfish are scavengers. They have rough tongues that can scrape the flesh off dead animals. Some fish eat different things at different times of year. The arapaima fish in the Amazon eats fish most of the time. When the forest is flooded and it finds itself swimming among trees, it eats fruit.

*Some fish eat very specific food. Parrotfish, like this one, eat only coral from a **coral reef**. It scrapes off bits of coral using the hard teeth in its beak-like mouth.*

Senses

Fish use different **senses** for finding their food. Pike have very good eyesight to spot prey. Great white sharks can smell tiny amounts of blood from dead or injured animals hundreds of metres away. Catfish have **barbels** (that look like cats' whiskers). These taste the water to find crabs and other shellfish to eat.

How do fish grow up in safety?

One way that fish avoid the many **predators** that try to eat them is by using camouflage (shapes, patterns or colours on their bodies that help them blend into the background so that predators don't notice them).

In disguise

Some fish are simply coloured like the rocks they swim and rest among. Flatfish, plaice and rays are sandy coloured. They also have flat bodies that make them very difficult to see when they lie on the seabed. Most fish are darker on top than on their belly. When a predator below looks up, the fish's pale belly cannot easily be seen against the light from the sky. From above, its dark back makes it hard to spot against the darker water below.

It is almost impossible to spot the sea dragon, a kind of seahorse. The shape, colour and flaps of skin on this unusual fish make it look like floating seaweed!

Defences

Many fish use built-in defences to **protect** them against predators. Some have armour made of tough scales or plates over their bodies. Weever fish have spiky **fins** that inject poison into anything that touches them. Electric eels give their enemies a nasty electric shock.

Clownfish hide among the stinging tentacles (long, wavy snake-like parts of some animals' bodies) of sea anemones in a coral reef. They do not get stung because their bodies are covered in a special protective slime and predators leave them well alone.

The pufferfish has scales shaped like spikes. To put off predators, this fish blows itself up with air into a horrid looking spiky ball!

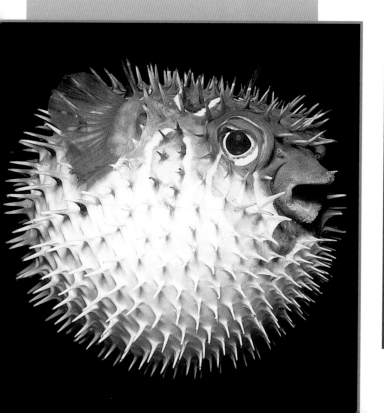

Different scales

Some fish, like catfish, have tough, leathery skin. Most fish have **scales** to protect the delicate skin beneath. Scales come in all sorts of different shapes and sizes. Carp have rounded scales that overlap like the tiles on a roof. Perch have scales with jagged 'teeth' on one end.

Keeping out of the way

As they get older, fish learn to keep out of the way of predators. Some do this by hiding. Sand eels burrow into the sand and some gobies live in holes made by prawns. Some fish escape danger by making a quick getaway. With its fins folded in, the sailfish is shaped like a smooth dart. It can shoot through the water at speeds of up to 110 km/h.

Flying fish have big pectoral (side) fins. They open these like wings and use them to glide swiftly over the surface of the water and out of reach of predators.

Safety in numbers

About one-fifth of all **species** of fish swim in **shoals** for protection. Anchovies and herrings form massive shoals sometimes called schools. When a predator attacks it is confused about which fish to take, and so catches fewer than it could.

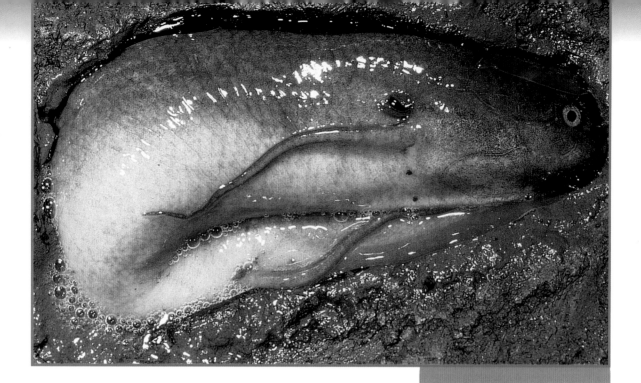

Avoiding the cold

In some places the freshwater in rivers
and ponds becomes freezing cold in
winter. To survive, some pond fish,
such as goldfish, stop feeding and
move to the bottom of the pond
where the water is warmer. Some river
fish **migrate** while it is cold – they swim
into warmer, deeper waters.

*A lungfish can
survive for up to
four years in its
nest. It comes out
when rain fills the
pond again.*

Sheltering from the heat

When heat makes ponds dry up, most fish die because they
cannot breathe without water passing over their **gills**. African
lungfish have lungs as well as gills. They burrow down into the
mud in the drying pond and make a nest of slime around
themselves. This keeps them moist as the mud around bakes
hard. They leave a narrow tunnel to the surface, and use their
lungs to breathe air through it.

When is a fish grown up?

A fish is 'grown up' when it is ready to start **breeding** – when it is able to **reproduce** and have young of its own. Some **species** of fish take longer to become adults than others. Most small fish, such as guppies, are grown up a few months after **hatching**, but whale sharks take about 25 years to become adults!

Other things, like temperature and competition for food, also changes the rate at which a fish grows. For example, if a tropical fish that usually lives in warm, shallow waters drifts into cooler, deeper seas, it may grow more slowly than its relatives. If many fish that are **carnivores** live in an area with a small amount of **prey**, individuals may grow more slowly because they have less to eat.

The great white shark is grown up at about ten years of age. It may live for 30 years and reach a length of 7 metres.

How do fish have babies?

To **reproduce** most **female** fish lay eggs in the water. Then a **male** fish of the same **species** swims over the eggs and releases **sperm** over them. When a sperm joins with an egg, the egg is **fertilized** – an **embryo** starts to grow inside it.

Finding a mate

In order to reproduce, fish must find or attract a **mate**. Some fish use **courtship** displays – colours or movements designed to attract a mate. Male salmon turn from silver to bright colours and develop hook-shaped jaws when it is time to **breed**. Male sticklebacks become more colourful and also do a special dance to encourage a female to lay her eggs.

To attract females, the male three-spined stickleback develops a bright red throat and belly. He builds a nest of weed and does a zigzag dance to lead females to lay their eggs there.

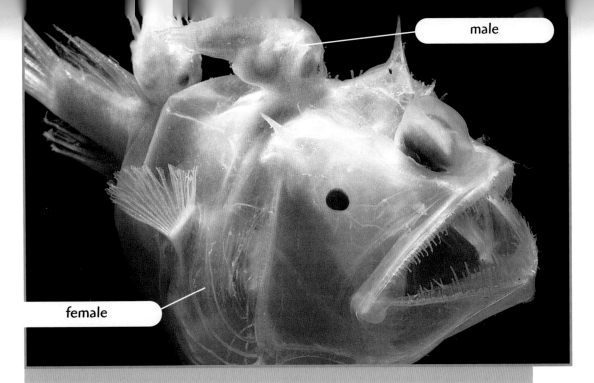

male

female

*In the darkness of the deep sea, the male anglerfish is attracted to a female's lure (light on her head). He attaches himself to her and lives as a **parasite**, feeding from her **blood supply**. He is always there to breed with her when she is ready.*

Mating territories

Some male fish set up **territories** to mate in. Territories are areas that are good places for laying eggs. Damselfish are fish that mostly live around **coral reefs**. A male damselfish makes a territory by clearing weed from an area of about 4 to 5 square metres. He uses courtship displays to attract females ready to mate. He chases away and attacks other males, other types of fish and sometimes even human divers.

Shoals

Fish that live in **shoals** don't have to find a mate. The female and male fish simply shed their eggs and sperm at the same time for fertilization to take place.

Breeding grounds

Male and female fish often meet up to breed at the same place year after year. For many species these places are a shallow part of the pond or river they live in. For others this involves long **migrations**. Adult European eels travel over 5000 km (3100 miles) from rivers, lakes and ponds where they grew up, to particular ocean breeding grounds. Their young return to live in the waters their parents came from.

Breeding seasons

Most fish breed at roughly the same time each year. In cooler parts of the world most fish reproduce in spring or early summer. The water is warmer then so the eggs and young develop more quickly. Also, there is more food around, such as insect **larvae**, for young fish to feed on.

Salmon live in the sea, but return to the rivers they were born in to breed. These salmon are jumping up a waterfall to continue their journey upstream.

Protecting eggs

Many animals like to eat fish eggs, so some fish have ways of
hiding their eggs. Some fish lay their eggs in dips in the sand or
gravel at the bottom of a river or pond. They may scoop out
the sand with their mouths or flick it away using their tails.
Most then cover their eggs with sand to hide them.

Others **protect** their eggs by staying
with them. Seahorses are unusual fish
with horse-shaped heads. A female
seahorse lays her eggs in a special pouch
on the male's front. The eggs remain
safe in the pouch until the young are
ready to hatch out and swim away.

*Californian grunions bury their
eggs high up the beach after
the highest tides. The eggs have
time to develop and hatch out
before the next very high tide
washes them out to sea.*

Egg cases

Some fish, such as the dogfish and the bullhead shark, lay just a few eggs. These have a good chance of survival because they are enclosed inside special containers. The cases are tough and protect the embryos inside as they grow. Fish often attach these egg cases to seaweed or rocks to prevent them being washed away. When the young fish is ready, it breaks out of the case and swims away.

Getting help

Some female fish find others to do the job of protecting their eggs. Bitterlings are river fish. The female has a long egg-laying tube that she uses to lay her eggs inside **shellfish** called mussels. The eggs then develop and hatch safely within the mussel's shell.

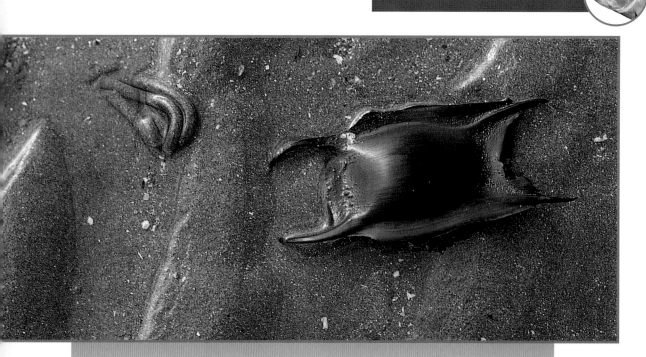

You sometimes see fish egg cases washed up on the shore after the babies inside have hatched. On the right is an egg case that contained the egg of the thornback ray.

How old do fish get?

An animal's life expectancy is the length of time it can live. Some fish can live for a long time. Cod can live for twenty years and pike and plaice can live for up to 50 years. Most fish **species** live for less than ten years. Sticklebacks are one kind of fish that only live for five years at most.

Most fish never reach their full life expectancy. They, like other animals, can only survive if they find enough food and water, and avoid dangers like fishing nets and **predators**. Young and adult fish face many different dangers throughout their lives.

*When adult salmon are about four or five years old, they return to the river where they were born. After **mating** and laying eggs, they die. They cannot feed in the river and they have no **energy** left for a return trip to the ocean.*

Fish are an important food for millions of people, but careless fishing can wipe out many species. Fishing nets with small holes catch very young fish. This means there are fewer youngsters to grow up into adults and have young of their own.

Sadly, too many of the colourful fish that live in **habitats** like this **coral reef** may not make it to adulthood. **Pollution**, careless use of fishing nets and building on coastlines all threaten the lives of fish in habitats in many parts of the world.

The circle of life

By the time an adult fish dies, it will have left behind many young fish. Some fish spawn (lay eggs) once or even twice each year. So the longer they live the more likely it is that some of their offspring will survive. A really big mother cod can live for 20 years and lay 10 million eggs every year. This means she could lay hundreds of millions of eggs in a lifetime!

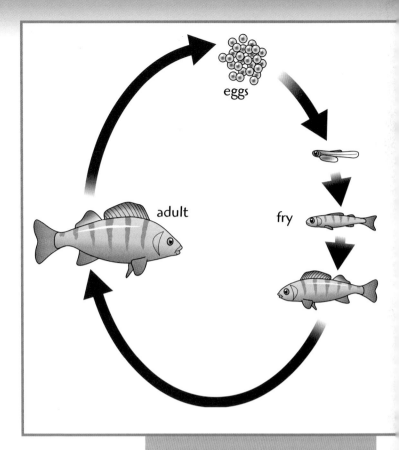

eggs

adult

fry

*Here you can see an adult trout laying eggs. The young fish that **hatch** out of eggs grow and eventually become adults, breed, grow old and die themselves – and so the circle of life continues.*

This diagram shows a typical fish life cycle – how a fish hatches from an egg and grows into an adult and then has young itself.

Fact file

What is ...

• *the largest fish?*

The largest fish in the world is the whale shark. It can grow to more than 12 metres long and weigh about 15 tonnes – that is twice as heavy as an African elephant.

• *the smallest fish?*

The smallest fish in the world is a goby that lives in the Indian Ocean. It is only 1 cm long.

• *the oldest fish?*

The record for the longest life that we know of goes to a North American lake sturgeon. It was 152 years old when it died.

• *the youngest fish?*

The shortest-lived fish is the annual fish from South America and Africa. It **hatches**, grows, **reproduces** and dies all in less than one year.

The goby fish is the smallest fish in the world. This goby is lying against some grape coral.

What fish lays the most eggs?

The record for the largest known number of eggs goes to a 1.5 m-long ling that laid over 28 million eggs at one time. A big cod can lay 7 to 10 million eggs a year. The eggs are tiny – 1000 cod's eggs weigh less than 1 gram.

Fish classification

Classification is the way scientists group living things together according to features they have in common. Scientists divide all the fish in the world into three main groups.

- The majority of fish are bony fish. These have bone skeletons, flat **scales** and **gills** protected by gill covers. The biggest group of bony fish is the perch-like fish. There are over 6000 different species of perch-like fish including perch, tuna, mackerel, bass and gobies.
- The second group is the cartilaginous fish. These have a skeleton made of **cartilage** or gristle. Their scales are pointed and their gills can be seen through slits on either side of the body. They are sharks, skates and rays.
- The smallest group is the jawless fish. These have no jaws and their skeletons are soft and made of cartilage. Lampreys and hagfish are jawless fish.

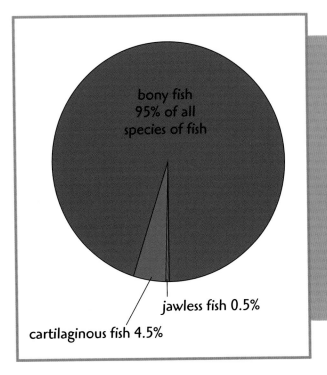

bony fish
95% of all
species of fish

jawless fish 0.5%

cartilaginous fish 4.5%

Most **species** of fish are bony fish – there are over 26,000. They can look as different as seahorses and marling, and live in seas, rivers and lakes all over the world. Only one out of every twenty spieces of all fish is a cartilaginous or jawless fish.

Glossary

barbels soft, thin, whisker-like features near the mouth of some kinds of fish. Fish use their barbels to feel things.

blood supply network of tubes that delivers blood to parts of the body

breed have babies

carnivore meat-eating animal

cartilage cartilage is softer than bone

coral reefs giant, rock-like structures made up of the skeletons of millions of tiny reef animals, joined together

courtship special behaviour that takes place before mating

embryo unborn or unhatched young

energy energy allows living things to do all they need to live and grow

female animal that can become a mother when it is grown up

fertilize when a sperm and an egg join and an embryo begins to grow

fin flap or fold of skin that helps fish to swim

fry very young fish

gills special parts for breathing

habitat place where a plant or animal lives. There are many different habitats in the world, such as a pond or a coral reef habitat.

hatch born from an egg

larva embryo that can live on its own, out of the egg, but not yet fully formed

male animal that can become a father when it is grown up

mate an animal's mate is an animal of the opposite sex that they can have young with. When a male and female animal mate, the female's eggs join with a male sperm, and an embryo starts to grow.

migrate/migration seasonal journey of animals to find food or a good place for breeding

muscles parts of the body that help to make the bones and body move

parasite animal (or plant) that lives on or inside another living thing. Parasites get food from the animal and may harm it.

plankton tiny plants and animals that float in water

pollution when something poisons or harms the environment (natural world)

predator animal that hunts and eats another animal

prey animal that is hunted and eaten by another animal

protect/protection keeping something safe

reproduce when plants and animals make young just like themselves

scales small, flat pieces that are hard like bone. These are on an animal's skin.

scavenger animal or bird that feeds on dead animals and rubbish

senses ways in which animals see, hear, touch, smell and taste things

shellfish sea animals that live inside shells, such as mussels, oysters, scallops and crabs

shoal large group of fish of the same kind that live and swim together

species group of living things that are similar in many ways and can reproduce together to produce healthy offspring (babies)

sperm male animals produce sperm. When a sperm joins with an egg from a female of the same species, the egg is fertilized.

territory area within a habitat that an animal or group of animals claims as its own and chases out uninvited visitors

yolk store of food inside an egg that feeds the embryo

Find out more

Books

Fish, Steve Parker (Dorling Kindersley, 1990)

Aquarium Fishes, Dick Mills (Kingfisher, 1989)

The Complete Aquarium, Peter Scott (Dorling Kindersley, 1991)

The World Encyclopedia of Fishes, A. Wheeler (Macdonald, 1985)

Websites

Great children's nature sites:
www.bbc.co.uk/reallywild/wildfacts
www.bbc.co.uk/nature

Great Barrier Reef fish:
www.nationalgeographic.com/kids

An introduction to plants and animals that live in different habitats:
www.enchantedlearning.com/biomes/

Index